SPARKS

BY

STINE

PAL PRESS/1987

For Margaret, then and now.

PAL PRESS, BOX 1124, OJAI, CA 93023   ISBN 0-9617782-0-2

MY POEM ← AND → ## MY DRAWING

A BOY FELL IN THE MUD.
SO DID A MAN.
(AND SO DID A DOG ONCE TOO)

QUESTIONS: WHAT IS THE DIFFERENCE BETWEEN MY DRAW-
ING AND REMBRANDT'S DRAWINGS?
AND WHAT IS THE DIFFERENCE BETWEEN MY
POEM AND THE POEMS OF EMILY DICKINSON?

GIVE UP?

ANSWER: MINE ARE A LOT BETTER.

SHOW BUSINESS

PERSON REACHING THROUGH THE GROSS TO GRASP THE SECRET OF BEAUTY.

Two views of Ernie

Ever wonder if Sartre had a dog?

CHRISTO'S CAT

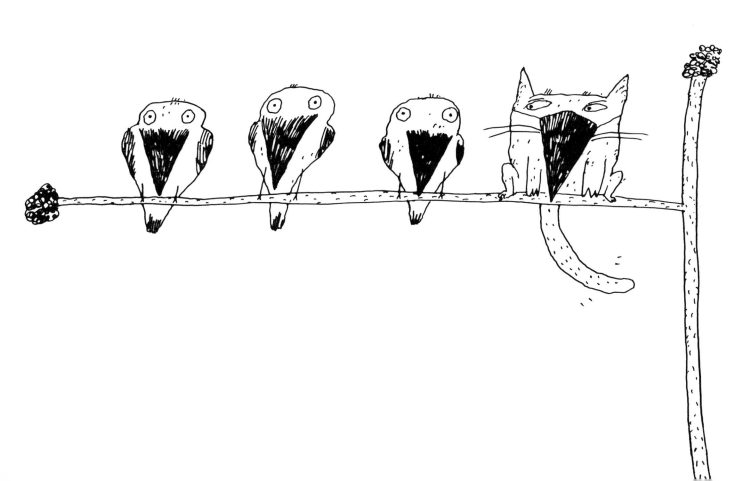

KILLER DOG

WORKINGS OF A COMMON DOG

NUDE DOGS

Mouse to Mouse
Resuscitation

Cat having
worked ~~real~~ very
hard to get
somewhere now
wondering where
it is she really
got.

Face to Face with
The Second Step.

CHILD SUPPORT

"HAS TELEVISION ADVERSELY AFFECTED MY CHILD?... DEFINITELY NOT, HE LOVES IT."

EVOLUTION

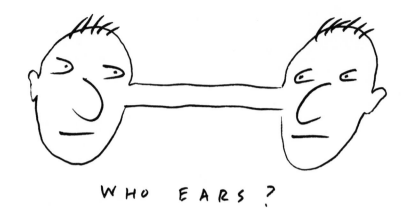

WHO EARS ?

WHO NOSE ?

WEDDING OF THE YEAR:
THE LOVELY MISS REPRE-
SENTATION TO GENERAL
COMMUNICATIONS.

Busybodies

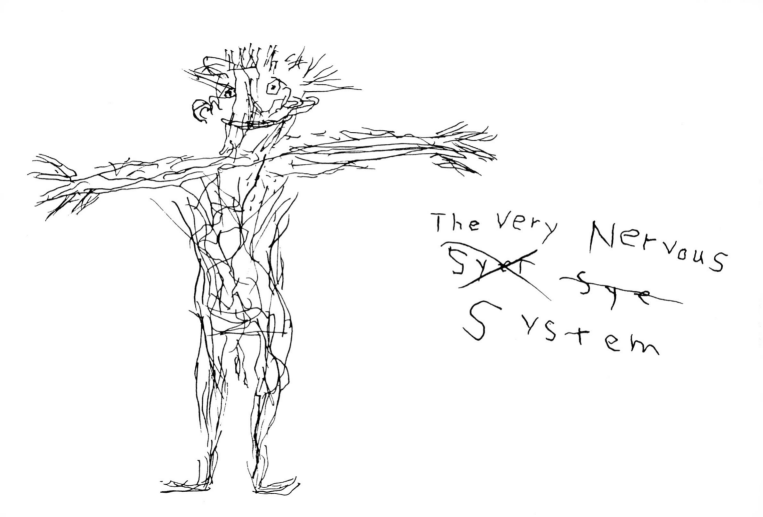

The Very Nervous ~~Syst~~ ~~Sye~~

System

HOW GLASSES ARE MADE.

High Tech: Lace-A-Face

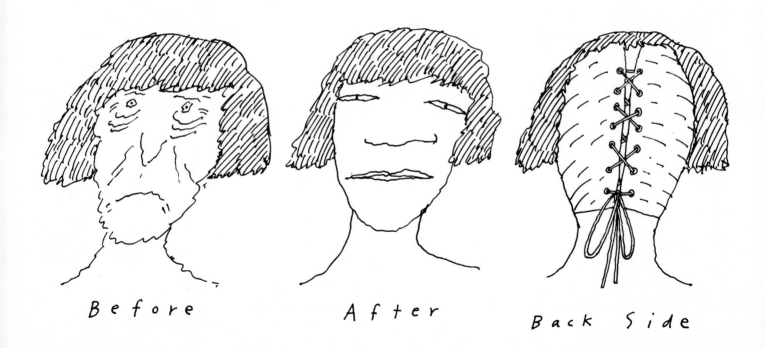

Before

After

Back Side

GLUE

Man Attempt-
ing to Stretch
the Limits of
His mind.

Man Struggling with
an Inability to Properly
Express Himself with
Words.

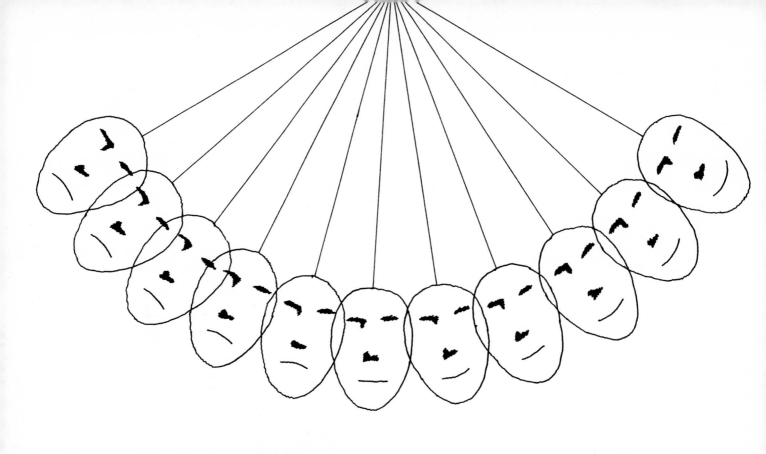

Mood Swing

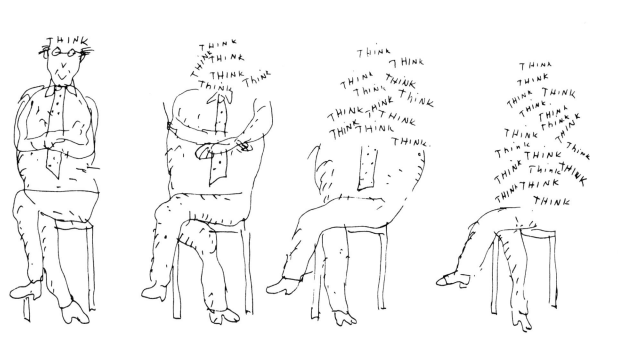

THE ALPHABET

For years Harry drew pictures with the wrong side of his brain. As a result he did bad dumb drawings that looked like pooh-pooh.

Then Harry took a class that taught him how to draw with the right side of his brain. And now they look more better.

S CREW

BALLS

DIG

NUKES

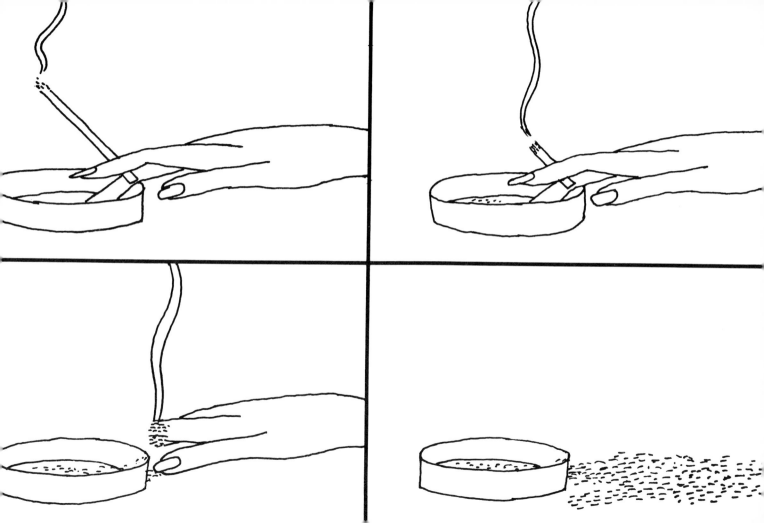

MAP OF THE WORLD

HEAVEN

HELL

HAWAII

Mating Buicks

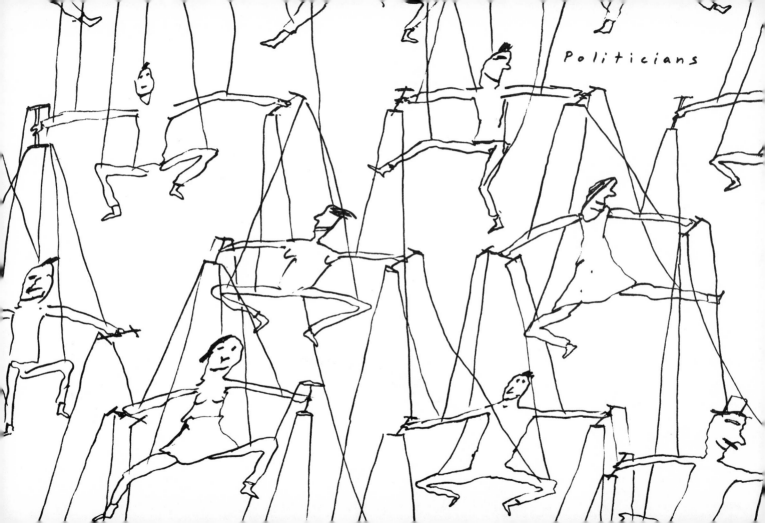

Politicians

MUSCLE MAN

MON

TUES

WEDS

THURS

FRI

SAT

SUN

MON

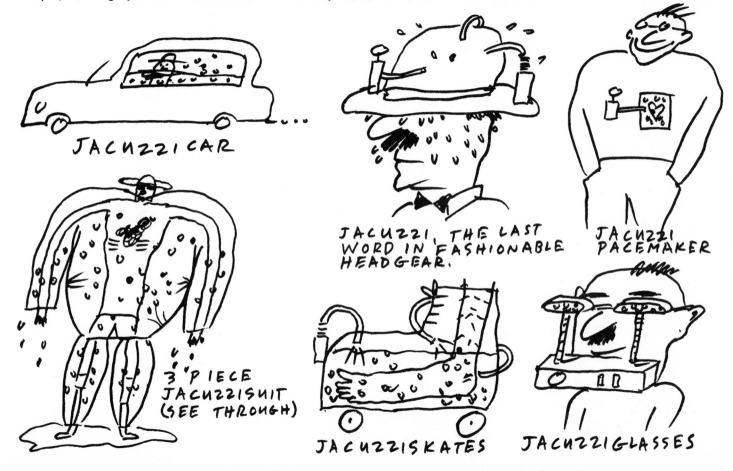

THINGS TO COME: CARS WILL CONTINUE TO GET SMALLER

LEAK SOUP

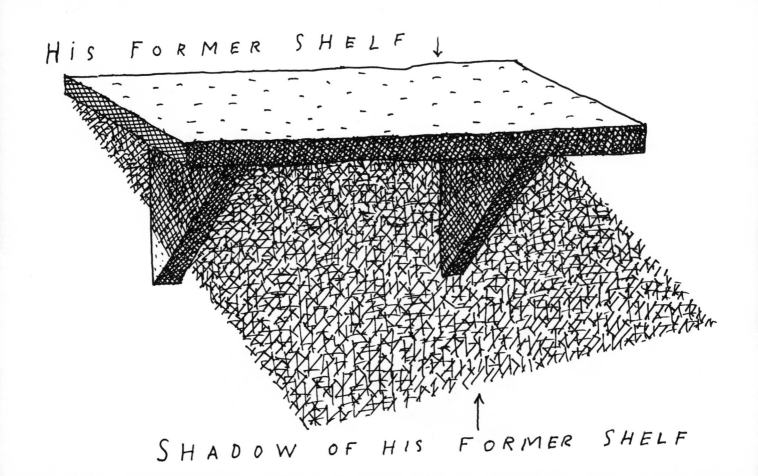

"when is it we're supposed to get our rocks off?"

Flying Saucers are seen everywhere...

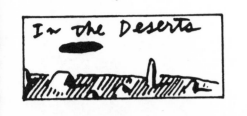

In the Deserts

In the Mountains

Near Big Cities

...But more are seen at Bob and Edna's than anywhere else.

UGH!

Things
That
Fly.

The Insured

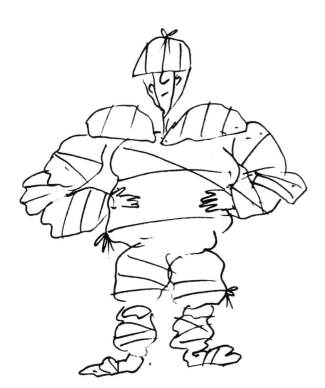

The Uninsured

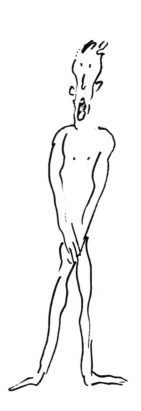

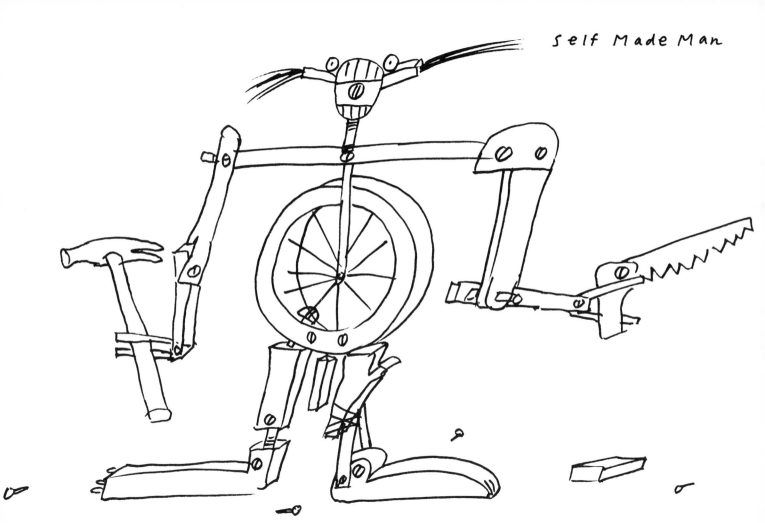

self Made Man

ANTO ISLAND

sneaker Birds

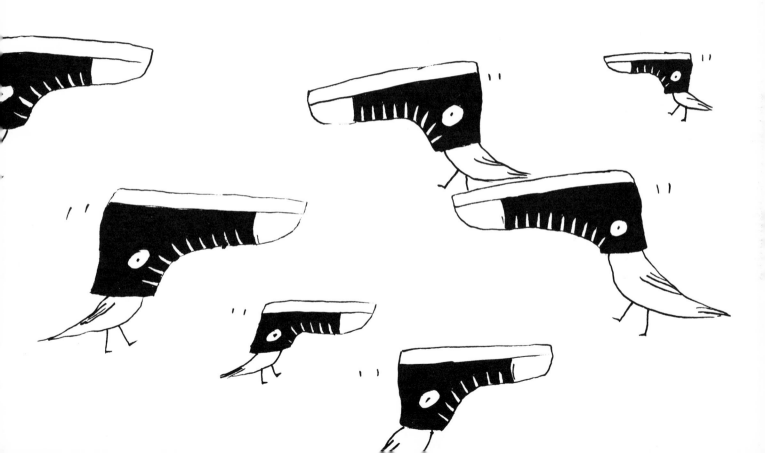

Actors and Dancers

"IN A NUTSHELL, WE WANT SOMETHING WITH MULTILEVEL MEANING, MYSTERY, AMBIGUITY, PROFUNDITY AND METAPHYSICAL ACCURACY... AND AT THE SAME TIME IT'S GOT TO BE DONE WITH HUMOR, IRONY AND A LIGHT TOUCH — SOMETHING EVERYONE CAN ENJOY."

'I SEE YOU'VE MOVED WILSON UP A NOTCH SINCE I WAS HERE LAST.'

"IN TODAY'S VIOLENT WORLD, FIGURING OUT THE SOUND OF ONE HAND CLAPPING SEEMS BESIDE THE POINT— WHAT, O WISE ONE, IS YOUR THOUGHT ON THE MATTER?"

HAIRY
KRISHNA

JESUS ENJOYING A GOOD CIGAR.

HARSH EDIT

BOOK

CHAOS AND ASSO.
DESTRUCTION INC.
DEATHCO
LOVE AND COMFORT CO.
I.T.C.
INTER NATIONAL TERRORIST CORP.

ONCE A THIEF, NOW A LAWMAN

1.

2.

Woman About to
Step On Some Branches
Which Are, in Reality,
Just Another Well
Made Trap.

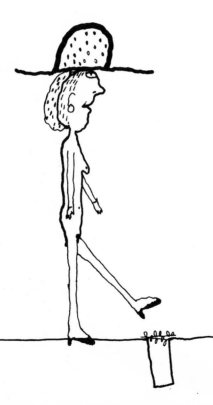

FAULT FINDERS

THE PERPETUAL ENIGMA

Mad Woman Trying
To Bury Delicate
Feelings Once And
For All.

yolanda conquered her fear of mice by living for years with a dirty rat.

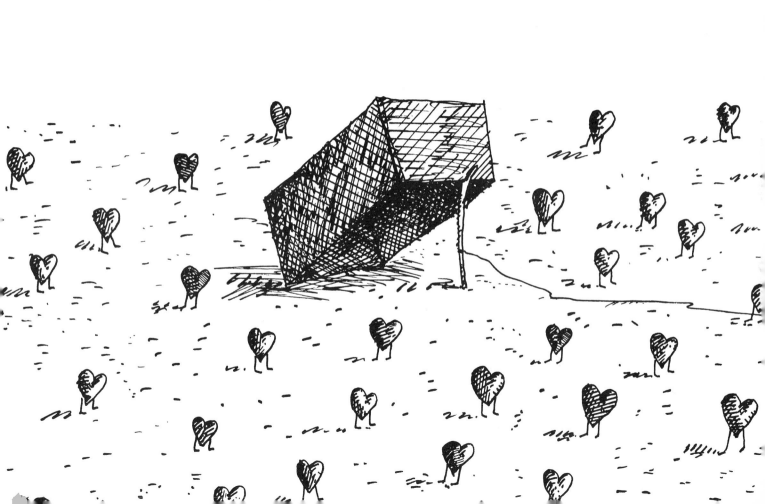

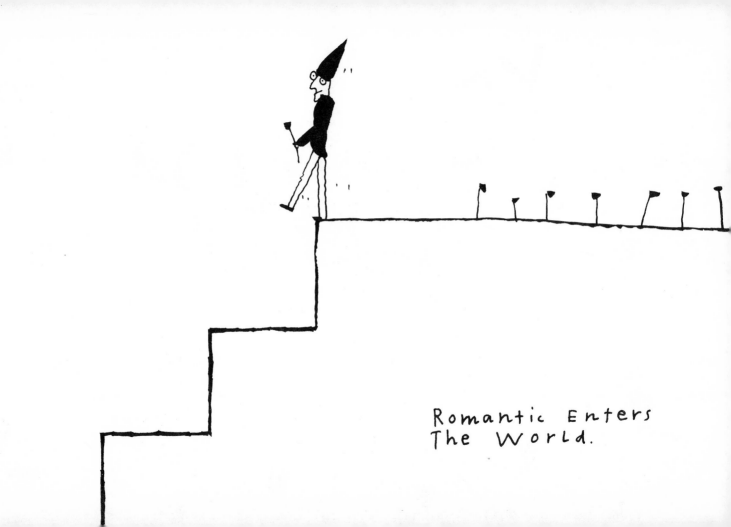

Romantic Enters
The World.

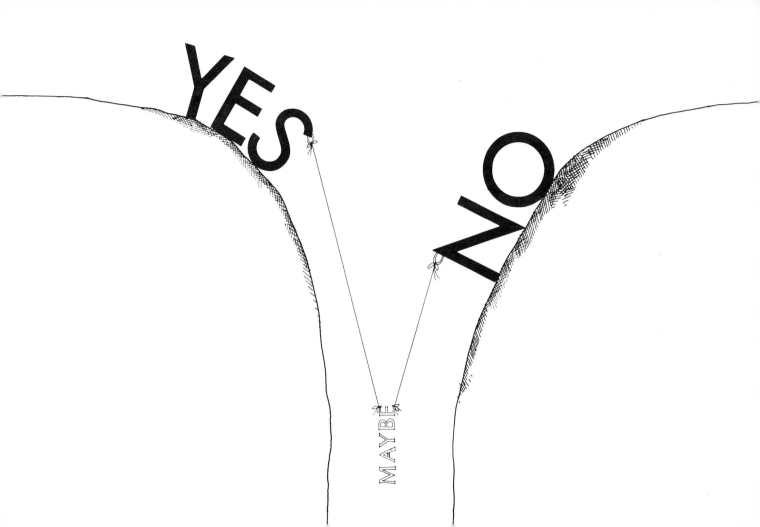

SUN SHINES EQUAL
ON OPPOSING FORCES

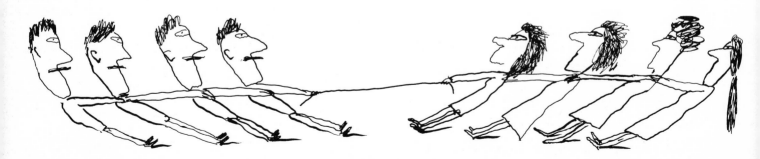

FALSE FRONTS

FACADES

Princess With Great Hopes
Kissing the Local Frog.

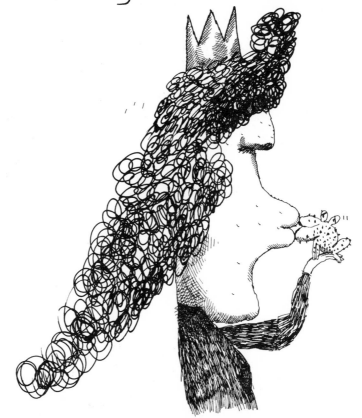

Ultimatum

THE HUSBAND THE WIFE THE LOVER THE PASSION THE KNIFE THE CRIME

THE GETAWAY THE VERDICT THE SENTENCE THE END.

THE CAPTURE THE TRIAL THE EVIDENCE

MADE FOR
EACH OTHER

Traces of a Reckless Affection.

Her first steps, though cautious, began immediately to reinforce her faith in greater possibilities.

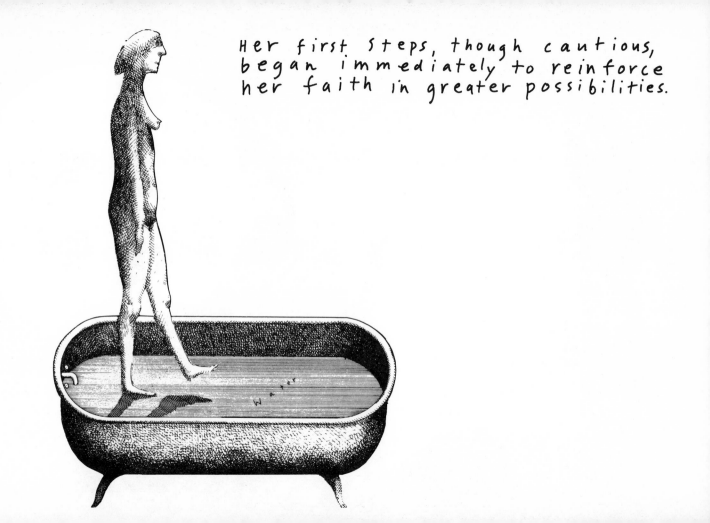

Attention ALL Fish: How to EScape Being Trapped in a Net.

1. Get So Big you Bust the muther.

2. Get So Small you swim right Through.

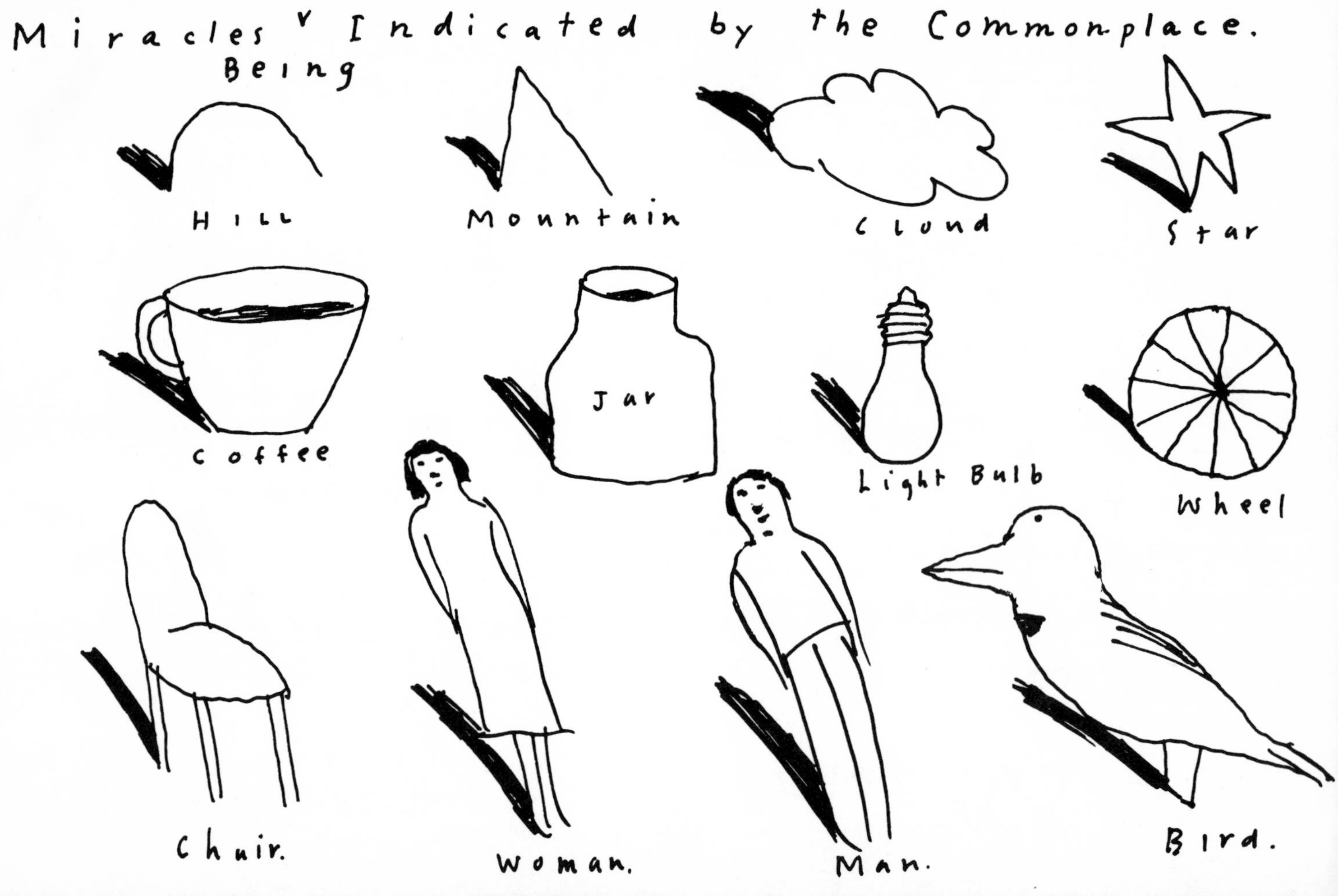

Miracles Indicated by the Commonplace. Being

Hill

Mountain

Cloud

Star

Coffee

Jar

Light Bulb

Wheel

Chair.

Woman.

Man.

Bird.

who made
the wind
and Rain?

who made
all the plants
and all the
creatures?

who made
Time and
space?

Who made
Day and
Night?

who made
Heaven and
Hell?

who made
the earth
and all the
Shining Stars?

You Guessed it!

Mr. and Mrs. Chet Ong
in their spare time be-
tween March 3, 1936 and
April 14, 1941.

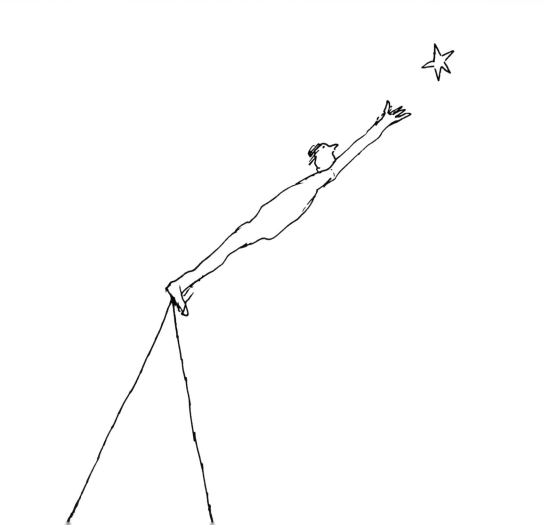